LLB

Land Law
Suggested Solutions

UNIVERSITY OF LONDON
June Examination 1992

GW00494956

HLT Publications

HLT PUBLICATIONS
200 Greyhound Road, London W14 9RY

Examination Questions © The University of London 1992
Solutions © The HLT Group Ltd 1992

ISBN 0 7510 0200 3

British Library Cataloguing-in-Publication.

A CIP Catalogue record for this book is available from the British Library.

Printed and bound in Great Britain.

Contents

Acknowledgement   v

Introduction   vii

Examination Paper   3

Suggested Solutions
    Question 1   11

    Question 2   17

    Question 3   23

    Question 4   29

    Question 5   35

    Question 6   39

    Question 7   45

    Question 8   53

Acknowledgement

The questions used are taken from past University of London LLB (External) Degree examination papers and our thanks are extended to the University of London for the kind permission which has been given to us to use and publish the questions.

Caveat:

The answers given are not approved or sanctioned by the University of London and are entirely our responsibility.

They are not intended as 'Model Answers', but rather as Suggested Solutions.

The answers have two fundamental purposes, namely:

a) To provide a detailed example of a suggested solution to examination questions, and

b) To assist students with their research into the subject and to further their understanding and appreciation of the subject of Laws.

Note:

Please note that the solutions in this book were written in the year of the examination for each paper. They were appropriate solutions at the time of preparation, but students must note that certain caselaw and statutes may subsequently have changed.

Introduction

Why choose HLT publications

Holborn College has earned an International reputation over the past ten years for the outstanding quality of its teaching, Textbooks, Casebooks and Suggested Solutions to past examination papers set by the various examining bodies.

Our expertise is reflected in the outstanding results achieved by our students in the examinations conducted by the University of London, the Law Society, the Council of Legal Education and the Associated Examining Board.

The object of Suggested Solutions

The Suggested Solutions have been prepared by College lecturers experienced in teaching to this specific syllabus and are intended to be an example of a full answer to the problems posed by the examiner.

They are not 'model answers', for at this level there almost certainly is not just one answer to a problem, nor are the answers written to strict examination time limits.

The opportunity has been taken, where appropriate, to develop themes, suggest alternatives and set out additional material to an extent not possible by the examinee in the examination room.

We feel that in writing full opinion answers to the questions that we can assist you with your research into the subject and can further your understanding and appreciation of the law.

Notes on examination technique

Although the SUBSTANCE and SLANT of the answer changes according to the subject-matter of the question, the examining body and syllabus concerned, the TECHNIQUE of answering examination questions does not change.

You will not pass an examination if you do not know the substance of a course. You may pass if you do not know how to go about answering a question although this is doubtful. To do well and to guarantee success, however, it is necessary to learn the technique of answering problems properly. The following is a guide to acquiring that technique.

1 Time

All examinations permit only a limited time for papers to be completed. All papers require you to answer a certain number of questions in that time, and the questions, with some exceptions carry equal marks.

It follows from this that you should never spend a disproportionate amount of time on any question. When you have used up the amount of time allowed for any one question STOP and go on to the next question after an abrupt conclusion, if necessary. If you feel that you are running out of time, then complete your answer in *note form*. A useful way of ensuring that you do not over-run is to write down on a piece of scrap paper the time at which you should be starting each part of the paper. This can be done in the few minutes before the examination begins and it will help you to calm any nerves you may have.

2 Reading the question

It will not be often that you will be able to answer every question on an examination paper. Inevitably, there will be some areas in which you feel better prepared than others. You will prefer to answer the questions which deal with those areas, but you will never know how good the questions are *unless you read the whole examination paper*.

You should spend *at least* 10 MINUTES at the beginning of the examination reading the questions. Preferably, you should read them more than once. As you go through each question, make a brief note on the examination paper of any relevant cases and/or statutes that occur to you even if you think you may not answer that question: you may well be grateful for this note towards the end of the examination when you are tired and your memory begins to fail.

3 Re-reading the answers

Ideally, you should allow time to re-read your answers. This is rarely a pleasant process, but will ensure that you do not make any silly mistakes such as leaving out a 'not' when the negative is vital.

4 The structure of the answer

Almost all examination problems raise more than one legal issue that you are required to deal with. Your answer should:

i) *identify the issues raised by the question*

This is of crucial importance and gives shape to the whole answer. It indicates to the examiner that you appreciate what he is asking you about.

This is at least as important as actually answering the questions of law raised by that issue.

The issues should be identified in the first paragraph of the answer.

ii) *deal with those issues one by one as they arise in the course of the problem*

This, of course, is the substance of the answer and where study and revision pays off.

iii) *if the answer to an issue turns on a provision of a statute, CITE that provision briefly, but do not quote it from any statute you may be permitted to bring into the examination hall*

Having cited the provision, show how it is relevant to the question.

iv) *if there is no statute, or the meaning of the statute has been interpreted by the courts, CITE the relevant cases*

'Citing cases' does not mean writing down the nature of every case that happens to deal with the general topic with which you are concerned and then detailing all the facts you can think of.

You should cite *only* the most relevant cases – there may perhaps only be one. No more facts should be stated than are absolutely essential to establish the relevance of the case. If there is a relevant case, but you cannot remember its name, it is sufficient to refer to it as 'one decided case'.

v) *whenever a statute or case is cited, the title of statute or the name of the case should be underlined*

This makes the examiner's job much easier because he can see at a glance whether the relevant material has been dealt with, and it will make him more disposed in your favour.

vi) *having dealt with the relevant issues, summarise your conclusions in such a way that you answer the question*

A question will often say at the end simply 'Advise A', or B, or C, etc. The advice will usually turn on the individual answers to a number of issues. The point made here is that the final paragraph should pull those individual answers together *and actually give the advice required.* For example, it may begin something like: 'The effect of the answer to the issues raised by this question is that one's advice to A is that ...'

vii) *related to (vi), make sure at the end that you have answered the question*

For example, if the question says 'Advise A', make sure that is what your answer does. If you are required to advise more than one party, make sure that you have dealt with all the parties that you are required to and no more.

5 *Some general points*

You should always try to get the examiner on your side. One method has already been mentioned – the underlining of case names, etc. There are also other ways as well.

Always write as *neatly* as you can. This is more easily done with ink than with a ball-point.

Avoid the use of violently coloured ink eg turquoise; this makes a paper difficult to read.

Space out your answers sensibly: leave a line between paragraphs. You can always get more paper. At the same time, try not to use so much paper that your answer book looks too formidable to mark. This is a question of personal judgment.

NEVER put in irrelevant material simply to show that you are clever. Irrelevance is not a virtue and time spent on it is time lost for other, relevant, answers.

EXAMINATION PAPER

UNIVERSITY OF LONDON
LLB EXAMINATION
PART I
for External Students

LAND LAW

Thursday, 4 June 1992: 10.00 to 1.00

Answer FOUR of the following EIGHT questions.

1. Distinguish a lease from a licence. To what extent is the distinction important today?

2. Last year Michael inherited a flat in London with 65 years of the lease unexpired. As Michael already had a house of his own in London, he decided to have the flat sold and he left the flat empty pending sale. Subsequently the landlords, Limetree Properties Ltd, sent a section 146 notice to the flat stating that the tenant was in breach of a) the covenant to keep the windows clean, b) the covenant to repaint the front door and the window frames before 1 January 1992 and c) the covenant not to place a window box on the window sill. Michael never saw the notice and two weeks later the landlords peaceably re-entered the flat and changed the locks.

    Advise Michael.

3. Alf and Bert own adjoining farms and from January 1972 Alf has used a rough track leading from his farm over Bert's land to the public road. The surface of the track made it only suitable for use by farm vehicles and when the weather was bad, the track was hardly passable at all. Alf and Bert were friends, and Bert never objected to Alf's use of the track. However, in 1990 Alf and Bert quarrelled and when, in April 1991, Alf began work paving the track with a view to making it suitable for passage by all kinds of vehicles, Bert wrote to Alf withdrawing 'the permission I gave you to use the track' and erected a fence barring access to the track from Alf's farm.

    Advise Alf.

3

4. In 1990 Henry bought a house to live in with his girlfriend, Joanna. The house was conveyed into Henry's sole name, but he agreed orally with Joanna that she was to have a 50% beneficial interest in the house. The purchase price was £50,000; Henry provided £5,000 from his savings, Henry's father lent him a further £15,000 and Henry borrowed the remaining £30,000 from the Savewell Bank in whose favour he executed a charge of the property expressed to be by way of legal mortgage. In 1991 Henry lost his job and began to fall badly into arrears with his mortgage repayments. Joanna has now left him and the bank is pressing him to repay his debt even though he is confident that he will find a well paid job within the near future.

    Henry would like to know:

    a) what his position would be if the bank applied to the court for a possession order;

    b) whether he would have any remedy if in the exercise of its power of sale the bank sold the house by private contract for less than its market value; and

    c) how the proceeds of sale would be disposed of.

    Advise Henry.

5. 'The purpose of section 70(1)(g) of the Land Registration Act 1925 was to make applicable to registered land the same rule for the protection of persons in actual occupation of land as had been applied in *Hunt* v *Luck*.'

    Explain this statement and consider the extent to which it is accurate.

6. Old Mr Jones, feeling that he would not be able to look after himself for very many more years, wrote to Mary, his unmarried daughter, suggesting that she come and live near him. He offered to buy her a flat to live in. Mary accepted the offer; she gave up her job and her council flat and moved into the flat her father had bought for her. The flat was conveyed into her father's name and he paid the whole of the purchase price. When Mary suggested that she would like the flat to be in her name, he dismissed the idea as absurd because, as he said, 'I am leaving everything to you in my will anyway'. Mr Jones paid all the outgoings on the flat and Mary paid nothing for the use of the flat. Mary found a part-time job and visited her father daily. This

arrangement continued happily for two years when Mr Jones died, leaving all his estate to charity. Now his executors seek possession of the flat.

Advise Mary.

Would your advice be any different if Mary had provided one-tenth of the purchase price of the flat?

7. Alan owned Blackacre and the adjoining Whiteacre, and in 1960 he sold Blackacre to Douglas who covenanted with Alan and his successors-in-title a) not to let the property fall into disrepair and b) not to use the property for business purposes.

    On the assumption that the land is unregistered, consider how far these covenants will be enforceable

    a) by a lessee of Whiteacre against Douglas;

    b) by Alan against an adverse possessor of Blackacre; and

    c) by a purchaser of Whiteacre against a purchaser of Blackacre.

8. Mike, Pat, Rob and Saul formed a pop group and decided to buy a house together situated near the recording studios. All four of them contributed equally to the purchase price and the house was conveyed into the joint names of Mike, Pat and Rob; Saul was aged 17 at the time of the conveyance. The pop group was not a success and in 1990 Mike sold his interest in the house to Pat. Shortly afterwards Rob wrote to Pat offering to sell him his interest for a certain price. Pat replied that he would be happy to purchase Rob's interest, but that the price was too high. Before any negotiations took place Rob was killed in a motor accident. Saul now wishes the house to be sold whereas Pat wishes to continue living there.

    Saul would like to know whether he can force a sale of the house and, if so, how the proceeds would be divided.

    Advise Saul.

SUGGESTED SOLUTIONS

Question 1

Distinguish a lease from a licence. To what extent is the distinction important today?

Suggested Solution to Question 1

General comment

A slight variation on the typical lease/licence question as it is neither solely about *Street* v *Mountford* nor licences as interests in land. The good candidate will cover both these issues in order to answer the question.

Skeleton solution

- Define lease and licence.
- Security of tenure.
- Exclusive possession.
- *Street* v *Mountford*.
- Protection against third party purchasers.
- Licence coupled with interest.
- Licences and constructive trusts.
- Estoppel licences.

Suggested solution

A lease is a document which creates a term of years in land, in other words it creates an interest in land – a proprietary right. Leases can be legal, ie made by deed in accordance with s52 Law of Property Act (LPA) 1925, or by parol, if they take effect in possession for a term not exceeding three years at the best rent reasonably obtainable (s54 LPA 1925). Licences on the other hand are, generally, merely personal rights giving no interest in land.

The distinction is of fundamental importance in relation to occupancy of residential premises because of the differing degrees of protection afforded to lessees and licensees. In short, lessees are afforded security of tenure whereas licensees are not. If a lease is found to exist the tenant will have the protection of the Protection from Eviction Act 1977, the Rent Act 1977 and the Housing Act 1988. The former governs the periods of notice to quit and the latter two give the tenant valuable rights in terms of security of tenure and the devolution of tenancies. For instance, under both the Rent Act and the Housing Act (with the exception of the assured shorthold tenancy under the latter) a tenant can only be removed from the premises if the landlord can show a mandatory or discretionary ground for possession. Until that time the tenant remains in possession. Similarly, a tenancy can

11

be succeeded to twice under the Rent Act (in favour of a spouse and then members of the tenant's family) and once under the Housing Act. The Rent Act tenant also has valuable rights in relation to rent assessment, whereby rents are subject to review by an adjudication officer.

Licensees on the other hand have no security of tenure, or rent control. They can be removed from the premises following a valid notice to quit, and there is no statutory control of rents. Not surprisingly in the light of the above there has been a continuous battle between landlords, who have constantly tried to create licences out of leases, and tenants who claim the latter. As a result of *Street* v *Mountford* (1), a standard test became applicable in deciding whether an agreement was a lease or not – if the agreement gave the occupant exclusive possession, for a term and at a rent, it was a lease despite any label to the contrary. Subsequent cases have refined that approach and it is now relevant to look not just to the agreement itself but the parties intentions at the time of its making, and how they operated the agreement in practice: *Antoniades* v *Villiers* (2). As a result of these cases certain propositions have emerged. Firstly, in cases of multiple occupancy licences can still exist if there is an absence of the four unities: *AG Securities* v *Vaughan* (2).

Secondly, in exceptional circumstances licences will exist despite the occupant's exclusive possession, eg where the occupant is in possession pursuant to a contract of employment or pending conveyance of the property to him, or pursuant to a local authority's statutory duties. On balance, however, the practice has been to favour the tenant by finding a lease with all its concomitant rights.

The distinction is also important in relation to protection against third parties. A lease is a legal estate in land and if over 21 years and legal, in an area subject to the Land Registration Act 1925, it will be registered as title. If it is legal and under 21 years it will take effect as an overriding interest under s70(1)(k), and is not capable of being overreached. If it is not made by deed and is an equitable lease of any duration, then it can be protected by the entry on the register as a minor interest or, failing that, as an overriding interest under s70(1)(g), although this can be overreached: *City of London Building Society* v *Flegg* (3). By contrast, a licence cannot be protected as title or a minor interest and cannot fall within s70(1)(g) as it is not an interest in land. In the case of land within the ambit of the Land Charges Act 1925, the legal lease will bind 'in rem' and the equitable one can be registered as a C(iv) land charge (estate contract). The licence, on the other hand, has no measure of protection and is not capable of binding third parties.

However, it must not be thought that the licence has no value whatsoever. It has always been recognised that a licence, coupled with an interest or profit, is capable of binding third parties if properly registered. Similarly, some cases of recent origin, eg *Binions* v *Evans* (4), have held that in appropriate cases a purchaser who has knowledge of a contractual licence will be bound by a constructive trust. Others have taken the view that contractual licences have the status of an equity in land (see *Errington* v *Errington* (5), although this was rejected obiter in *Ashburn Anstalt* v *Arnold* (6), where the court preferred the traditional view that contractual licences are personal only: see *King* v *David Allen Billposting* (7).

More importantly, however, estoppel licences have been recognised as giving rise to an interest in land capable of binding third parties. These come about on normal estoppel principles, viz, representation and reliance, and are commonly shown by expenditure on the land of another (*Inwards* v *Baker* (8)), mutual benefit and burden (*Ives* v *High* (9)) and acquiescence (*Plimmer* v *Mayor of Wellington* (10)). In any event once the estoppel has arisen the task for the court is how best to satisfy it. Two of the options open to the court are to grant the licensee a life interest (*Inwards*) or to convey the fee simple to him (*Pascoe* v *Turner* (11)). Like all estoppels, it will bind everyone except the purchaser for value without notice.

Clearly, in terms of residential occupation in the rented sector, the distinction between a lease and a licence is of fundamental importance. Whereas it might be said that the courts favoured the occupant following *Street* v *Mountford*, the Housing Act has redressed the balance somewhat by the introduction of the assured short-hold tenancy. That said, the licence in other areas is afforded some value, not least through the concept of estoppel.

References

(1)   [1985] AC 809
(2)   [1988] 3 WLR 1205
(3)   [1988] AC 54
(4)   [1972] Ch 359
(5)   [1952] 1 KB 290
(6)   (1987) 2 EGLR 71
(7)   [1916] 2 AC 54
(8)   [1965] 2 QB 29
(9)   [1967] 2 QB 279
(10)   (1884) 9 App Cas 699
(11)   [1979] 1 WLR 431

Question 2

Last year Michael inherited a flat in London with 65 years of the lease unexpired. As Michael already had a house of his own in London, he decided to have the flat sold and he left the flat empty pending sale. Subsequently the landlords, Limetree Properties Ltd, sent a section 146 notice to the flat stating that the tenant was in breach of a) the covenant to keep the windows clean, b) the covenant to repaint the front door and the window frames before 1 January 1992 and c) the covenant not to place a window box on the window sill. Michael never saw the notice and two weeks later the landlords peaceably re-entered the flat and changed the locks.

Advise Michael.

Suggested Solution to Question 2

General comment
A question which requires some thought and a particular knowledge of the mechanics of s146 notices. Candidates would be expected to deal with the contents of a s146 notice and its service, particularly where one of the covenants requires some repairs. The issue of relief from forfeiture has to be addressed in the light of *Billson* v *Residential Properties*.

Skeleton solution
- Running of leasehold covenants – *Spencer's Case*.
- Contents of s146 LPA 1925 notices.
- Leasehold Property (Repairs) Act 1938.
- Service of s146 notices.
- Relief from forfeiture – *Billson* v *Residential Apartments Ltd*.

Suggested solution
By virtue of his inheritance Michael has obtained a term of years for a period of 65 years, and, as successor in title to the original tenant, he will take the benefit and the burden of all the covenants which touch and concern the land: see *Spencer's Case* (1). Consequently the three covenants, being more than personal covenants, are binding on Michael.

The landlord has served a s146 notice alleging breach of the covenants. It is necessary to see whether that notice is valid. In order for the landlord to forfeit the lease in this manner there must be a forfeiture clause in the lease. I assume that this is the case. According to s146, the notice must include a statement of the breaches, require them to be remedied and compensation. However, the cases have relaxed these requirements in appropriate circumstances.

As required by the section, the notice does specify the breaches complained of. It should have required those breaches to be remedied, but, and as far as the cases go, the notice need only require breaches of positive covenants to be remedied – in this case covenants (a) and (b): see *Scala House and District Properties* v *Forbes* (2). As regards covenant (c), this is negative in nature, and the view expressed in *Governors of Rugby School* v *Tannahill* (3), was that negative covenants were irremediable and, therefore it was not necessary for the s146 notice to require them to be remedied. In the later case of *Expert Clothing Service and Sales Ltd* v *Hillgate House*

17

Ltd (4), the Court of Appeal suggested that a negative covenant was capable of remedy. If this is correct then the landlord should have required covenant (c) to be remedied – which, after all, would be a comparatively simple task, namely, removing the window box.

If the landlord required compensation in respect of the breaches then he must have specified this in the notice. An additional element must be included in the s146 notice as the Leasehold Property (Repairs) Act 1938 applies, viz, there is a repairing covenant (covenant (b)) in a lease which was originally for a term in excess of seven years and three years remain unexpired. Under the 1938 Act, the s146 notice should have drawn Michael's attention to his rights under the Act.

Assuming that the s146 notice contains the right elements, it is also necessary to look at whether it has been served correctly. Section 146 notices are served by sending them to the lessee or person interested, or by sending them to the demised premises by registered or recorded delivery, or by attaching it to the demised premises. In this case the letter was sent to the flat so, prima facie, that would be good service on Michael. However, as the notice concerns breach of a repairing covenant s18 Landlord and Tenant Act 1927 should have been complied with. Section 18 requires that service of the notice must be *known* to the lessee, under-lessee or the person who last paid rent. In our case Michael (the new lessee) did not know of the notice and therefore it is invalid.

Insofar as the landlord purported to re-enter pursuant to the notice several points have to be made. Firstly, s18 Landlord and Tenant Act 1927 states that reasonable interval must have elapsed between the date on which service was known to the appropriate person and the actual re-entry. Whether two weeks would be reasonable is a moot point even if it could be shown that Michael knew of the notice. Secondly, and more importantly, it is now settled as a result of the House of Lords' judgment in *Billson* v *Residential Apartments Ltd* (5), that a tenant can apply for relief from forfeiture under s146(2) whenever a landlord *has* re-entered pursuant to a s146 notice but without a court order – as is the case here. Therefore, following *Billson* it would be open to Michael to apply for relief against forfeiture.

In deciding whether to grant relief, the court will look at the gravity of the breach and all the circumstances of the case in order to see whether it is just and equitable to do so. On the facts breaches of covenants (a) and (c) are of a trivial nature, and whereas covenant (b) is not so trivial, it is not in the nature of breach of a user or assignment covenant. In the circumstances it is quite possible that the court will grant relief, and in doing so it can attach conditions, eg that Michael pay all, or part, of the landlord's expenses.

References
(1)   (1583) 5 Co Rep 16
(2)   [1974] QB 575
(3)   [1935] 1 KB 87
(4)   [1986] Ch 340
(5)   [1992] 1 All ER 141

Question 3

Alf and Bert own adjoining farms and from January 1972 Alf has used a rough track leading from his farm over Bert's land to the public road. The surface of the track made it only suitable for use by farm vehicles and when the weather was bad, the track was hardly passable at all. Alf and Bert were friends, and Bert never objected to Alf's use of the track. However, in 1990 Alf and Bert quarrelled and when, in April 1991, Alf began work paving the track with a view to making it suitable for passage by all kinds of vehicles, Bert wrote to Alf withdrawing 'the permission I gave you to use the track' and erected a fence barring access to the track from Alf's farm.

Advise Alf.

Suggested Solution to Question 3

General comment

Not a particularly difficult question on easements. The key issues to deal with are whether there is permission or acquiescence on the part of Bert, whether the limited time during which the path was useable is relevant and whether Alf can improve the path. Candidates who are aware of *Mills* v *Silver* should not be unduly troubled by this question.

Skeleton solution

* Definition of easement.

* Characteristics of easement – *Re Ellenborough Park*.

* Acquisition of easements generally.

* Prescription – acquiescence or permission – *Dalton* v *Angus* – nec vi, nec clam, nec precario – Prescription Act 1832 – 20 years' user – *Mills* v *Silver*.

* Maintenance or improvement of easements – *Mills* v *Silver*.

Suggested solution

An easement is a right in or over the land of another – it is a right 'in alieno solo'. Alf wishes to know whether he can continue to make use of the track across Bert's land. In order to be able to do so he must show that the track has the characteristics of an easement, and has been acquired as such.

The characteristics of an easement were laid down in *Re Ellenborough Park* (1) as follows. Firstly, there must be a dominant and servient tenement. The dominant tenement has the benefit of the alleged easement and the servient the burden. In this case Alf's farm is the dominant tenement and Bert's the servient.

Secondly, the easement must 'accommodate' the dominant tenement. In *Re Ellenborough Park* the court said that an easement would do so if it made the dominant tenement a 'better and more convenient property', eg if it increased the value of that property. It was also said in that case that there must be a sufficient nexus between the enjoyment of the easement and the dominant tenement; in other words the servient and dominant tenements must be proximate, but not necessary adjoining or adjacent, so as to enable the dominant tenement to derive a realistic benefit from the easement. On the facts it is clear that the nexus test is satisfied as the farms are adjoining, and it could also be argued that the use of a path over Bert's land increases the value of Alf's farm. In addition it must be shown that the easement accommodates the land (Alf's farm) as opposed to the person (Alf), as an easement is more than a mere personal right: see *Hill* v *Tupper* (2) and *Moody* v *Steggles* (3). As paths are the most common type of easement it may be safe to assume that the easement accommodates the land.

Thirdly, the dominant and servient land must be owned and occupied by different persons. This is clearly satisfied as Bert owns the servient land and Alf the dominant. Finally, the easement must be capable of forming the subject matter of grant – it must be a right which could have been granted by deed. For this to be satisfied there must be a capable grantor and grantee, and as there is nothing to suggest that Bert or Alf are subject to some incapacity at law there would be a grantor and grantee respectively. The right claimed as an easement also needs to be sufficiently definite and not a claim of privacy or view, as well as being in the nature of a recognised easement. Again these requirements are satisfied as a path in the nature of a right of way is one of the oldest recognised easements.

Thus the path across Bert's land is capable of being an easement in the form of a right of way in favour of Alf. However, whether Alf actually has an easement depends on whether he has acquired it in a manner recognised by law.

An easement can be acquired in several ways, most of which can be discounted here. There is no suggestion of an express grant of an easement by Bert in favour of Alf, nor is there likely to be an easement of necessity in the absence of Alf's farm being 'land-locked': see *Wong* v *Beaumont* (4) and *Nickerson* v *Barraclough* (5). Similarly, in the absence of a conveyance between Bert and Alf, s62 Law of Property Act 1925 and the doctrine in *Wheeldon* v *Burrows* (6) cannot apply. Therefore, if Alf has acquired an easement at all he will have done so by prescription.

A prescriptive easement can be acquired in three ways – common law prescription, lost modern grant, and under the Prescription Act 1832. All three are based on acquiescence and it is necessary to show that the servient owner knows of the use over his land by the dominant owner, has the power to stop it or sue in respect of it, and fails to do: *Dalton* v *Angus* (7). On the facts it would appear that these factors are satisfied as Bert knows of Alf's use of the track and only takes steps to stop it in 1991. All three types of prescription are also based on longer user as of right, without force, secrecy or permission (nec vi, nec clam, nec precario). These factors will now be considered in respect of the different types of prescription.

In order to successfully plead common law prescription, Alf would have to show that the path has been used across Bert's farm since time immemorial – 1189. Although the rule is deemed to be satisfied if the use can be shown to have existed throughout the memory of the oldest living inhabitant of the area, such a plea will fail even if the farms had existed since that time in view of the fact that the path has, apparently, only existed since 1972. Alf may have more success in pleading lost modern grant. This is essentially a fiction whereby 20 years' user or more as of right was presumed to arise from the grant of a deed which had since been lost: *Tehidy Minerals* v *Norman* (8). The difficulty for Alf here would be that he could not show 20 years' user as of right. Obviously until April 1991 there is 19 years and four months' user as of right, but since then user has been prevented by virtue of the fence across the path.

Alf's strongest case lies in pleading the Prescription Act 1832. Under s2 and s4 of the Act, 20 years' user as of right next before some suit or action without interruption must be shown. Several points must be considered here: is there 20 years' user in view of the fact that the path is not passable when the weather is bad?; has Alf used as of right?; and is there an interruption?

As to the first point, it was settled in *Mills* v *Silver* (9) that an easement in the form of right of way could come into existence notwithstanding the fact that the path in question could only be used in dry weather. As to the second point, Bert will no doubt seek to argue that he had given Alf permission to use the path back in January 1972 as indicated in his letter of April 1991; however, a distinction must be drawn between acquiescence which is the basis of prescription (*Dalton* v *Angus*) and permission. If there was true permission Alf cannot claim an easement, but if there was acquiescence or toleration it is not open for Bert to seek to grant permission ex post facto by his letter of April 1991.

The 20 year period can, of course, be defeated by an interruption provided that it lasts for at least one year and is known to the dominant owner who submits to it. Although it is reasonable to assume Alf knows of the existence of the fence, it is not clear whether he has submitted to it. In any event it will not be a valid interruption because the year of interruption will expire in April 1992, whereas the 20 years' user will expire four months earlier in January 1992, thereby enabling Alf to claim the easement.

Hence, Alf appears to have acquired a legal easement over Bert's farm by virtue of the Prescription Act 1832, which will entitle him to get a mandatory injunction requiring Bert to remove the fence. However, the easement is limited to the right to pass and re-pass along the track. In other words it does not give Alf the right to improve the track, merely to repair it, and insofar as Alf has commenced improvements by paving the track he has committed a trespass which will enable Bert to recover damages from him (see *Mills* v *Silver*).

References
(1)   [1956] Ch 131
(2)   (1863) 2 H & C 121
(3)   (1879) LR 12 Ch D 261
(4)   [1965] 1 QB 173
(5)   [1980] Ch 325
(6)   (1879) 12 Ch D 31
(7)   (1881) 6 App Cas 740
(8)   [1971] 2 QB 528
(9)   [1991] 2 WLR 324

Question 4

In 1990 Henry bought a house to live in with his girlfriend, Joanna. The house was conveyed into Henry's sole name, but he agreed orally with Joanna that she was to have a 50% beneficial interest in the house. The purchase price was £50,000; Henry provided £5,000 from his savings, Henry's father lent him a further £15,000 and Henry borrowed the remaining £30,000 from the Savewell Bank in whose favour he executed a charge of the property expressed to be by way of legal mortgage. In 1991 Henry lost his job and began to fall badly into arrears with his mortgage repayments. Joanna has now left him and the bank is pressing him to repay his debt even though he is confident that he will find a well paid job within the near future.

Henry would like to know:

a) what his position would be if the bank applied to the court for a possession order;

b) whether he would have any remedy if in the exercise of its power of sale the bank sold the house by private contract for less than its market value; and

c) how the proceeds of sale would be disposed of.

Advise Henry.

Suggested Solution to Question 4

General comment

A question which coupled the law of mortgages and trusts. As regards the bank seeking possession mention must be made of the Administration of Justice Acts. The case of *Cuckmere Brick* must be discussed in the context of the low sale price, and s105 Law of Property Act (LPA) 1925 as regards the distribution of proceeds. In dealing with the distribution of proceeds it is necessary to see whether Henry's father and Joanna can claim an interest in the house, and, consequently, in the proceeds. Constructive trusts, resulting trusts and proprietary estoppel should be considered in this context.

Skeleton solution

- Definition of mortgage.

- *Four Maids* v *Dudley Marshall*.

- Possession a prelude to sale – dwelling house – s36 Administration of Justice Act 1970 – s8 Administration of Justice Act 1973.

- *Cuckmere Brick Co Ltd* v *Mutual Finance Ltd* – mortgagee's duty of care on sale – negligence.

- Section 101 LPA 1925 – s103 LPA 1925 – distribution of proceeds: s105 LPA 1925.

- Interest for father – loan – *Re Sharpe*.

- Interest for Joanna – constructive or resulting trust.

Suggested solution

A mortgage is a security for a loan and can be either legal or equitable. In this case Savewell Bank have a legal mortgage in the form of a charge over the property. As legal mortgagee the bank have certain powers, namely of sale, to take possession, to foreclose and to appoint a receiver.

a) *Possession*

The bank are entitled to take possession of the house 'before the ink is dry on the mortgage' (*Four Maids* v *Dudley Marshall* (1)), unless they have expressly or impliedly excluded their right to do so (*Birmingham Citizens' Permament Building Society* v *Caunt* (2)). Should the bank wish to rely on these broad rights, possession will only be granted if it is equitable to do so: *Quennell* v *Maltby* (3). In reality however, possession is usually sought for two different reasons. Firstly, if the mortgagee does not wish to realise his security he may seek possession of the land with a view to intercepting the rents and profits from the land, and recovering his interest. Such a move is attended by liability on the basis of wilful default, in the sense that the mortgagee will be liable to the mortgagor not for the income he actually generates from the land, but for the income he *could* have generated from the land: *White* v *City of London Brewery* (4).

The second use of possession is as a prelude to sale, as the mortgagee will wish to obtain possession in order to sell with vacant possession. This appears to be the case here. In these circumstances there are several remedies open to Henry as the action concerns a dwelling house. Under s36 Administration of Justice Act 1970, the court may adjourn or suspend or postpone proceedings if the mortgagor could, within a reasonable time, pay off the arrears. The fact that Henry is confident that he will find a well paid job in the near future is a relevant consideration. On the assumption that the mortgage is an instalment mortgage, the court may treat as the sums owing only those instalments which are actually in arrear, even though the mortgage may require the whole of the outstanding balance to be paid upon default: s8 Administration of Justice Act 1973.

In the circumstances then it would be open to Henry to apply to the court under the Administration of Justice Act 1970 to postpone or suspend any order for possession sought by the bank.

b) *Sale at less than market value*

In the first place the bank, as mortgagee, has an absolute discretion as to the mode and time of sale. It can choose to sell by way of private treaty (as in this case) or by way of auction, and it is not obliged to wait until the market improves. However, once the bank decides to sell it is subject to certain duties. First, and foremost, it is clear from *Cuckmere Brick Co Ltd* v *Mutual Finance Ltd* (5) that a mortgagee is not a trustee for the mortgagor in respect of the power of sale. He is, however, a trustee in respect of how that power is exercised and accordingly owes a duty of care to the mortgagor or guarantor to obtain the best price upon sale: *Standard Chartered Bank* v *Walker* (6). Failure to do so will render the mortgagee liable to the mortgagor for the difference between the price he obtained and the price he could have obtained (*Cuckmere*).

c) *Proceeds of sale*

As the mortgage is by way of legal charge made by deed after 1881, the power of sale has arisen in favour of the bank (s101 LPA 1925), and in view of the fact that Henry is badly in arrear, one of the conditions making the power exercisable under s103 LPA 1925 has been satisfied. Upon sale being concluded the proceeds of sale will be distributed in accordance with s105 LPA 1925. Under that section, in the absence of any prior encumbrance, the costs and expenses of sale will be defrayed first, then the bank will take the mortgage monies owing to it, any balance will be paid to subsequent mortgagees if any, and if not, to the mortgagor (Henry). Should there be any prior encumbrances they will be paid first.

Assuming the proceeds of sale are sufficient to satisfy the mortgage debt and leave a balance, that balance is paid to the mortgagor (Henry). The question is whether Henry's father and Joanna are entitled to a share of that balance.

It is likely that the father will be entitled to a share in the balance by virtue of the loan he made to Henry. As it is a loan, it negatives any presumption of advancement or gift between father and son, and, according to *Re Sharpe* (7) and *Hussey* v *Palmer* (8), would give the father an interest in property pending repayment of the loan. In the circumstances Henry's father will be entitled to the repayment of his £15,000 loan.

On the other hand it is unlikely that Joanna will be able to claim a share in the proceeds. In the first place she has not made any direct financial contribution to the purchase of the house either by way of deposit or mortgage instalments, so as to establish a beneficial interest in her favour under a resulting or constructive trust (*Lloyds Bank* v *Rosset* (9)). Secondly, although she may be able to point to the oral agreement that she should have 50 per cent share in the house, she does not appear to have acted to her detriment upon that agreement so as to raise an interest under a trust or by way of estoppel in her favour: *Lloyds Bank* v *Rosset* and *Grant* v *Edwards* (10).

References
(1)   [1957] Ch 317
(2)   [1962] Ch 883
(3)   [1979] 1 WLR 318
(4)   (1889) 42 Ch D 327
(5)   [1971] Ch 949
(6)   [1982] 1 WLR 144
(7)   [1980] 1 WLR 219
(8)   [1972] 1 WLR 1286
(9)   [1990] 2 WLR 867
(10)   [1986] Ch 638

Question 5

'The purpose of section 70(1)(g) of the Land Registration Act 1925 was to make applicable to registered land the same rule for the protection of persons in actual occupation of land as had been applied in *Hunt* v *Luck*.'

Explain this statement and consider the extent to which it is accurate.

Suggested Solution to Question 5

General comment
A question which requires candidates to state what the rule in *Hunt* v *Luck* is, how it applies and then to compare it with s70(1)(g). The similarities and the differences between the two principles should be teased out. This is not a question for the student who either does not know what *Hunt* v *Luck* says or is unable to analyse it.

Skeleton solution
- Explanation of *Hunt* v *Luck* – explanation of doctrine of notice.
- Elements of s70(1)(g) LRA 1925.
- Need to investigate the land.
- Enquiries of persons on the land.
- Overreaching.

Suggested solution
The rule in *Hunt* v *Luck* (1) is intimately connected with the common law doctrine of notice. At common law the purchaser of land was bound by any equitable interest in land of which he had actual, constructive or imputed notice. The rule in *Hunt* can be expressed as follows; a purchaser of land must make enquiries of any person in possession of the land and if he fails to do so then any title he acquires will be subject to that of the person in possession. In short, the purchaser would be caught by constructive notice. In its original formulation the rule was only applicable to the interests of a tenant in possession, but was later extended to cover the interests of any person in possession.

Section 70(1)(g) applies in the context of the Land Registration Act 1925 and is one of the categories of overriding interest. As such it will not appear on the land certificate thereby shattering the 'mirror principle', and, as an overriding interest it is capable of binding a purchaser. In order for s70(1)(g) to be made out a person must be in actual occupation of the land (see *Epps* v *Esso Petroleum Co Ltd* (2)) with an interest in land capable of binding subsequent owners of the land, in other words, a proprietary interest as opposed to a personal one (*Williams & Glyn's Bank* v *Boland* (3)). Additionally he must not have concealed that interest upon enquiry being made of him.

35

In *Strand Securities* v *Caswell* (4), Lord Denning described s70(1)(g) as carrying the rule in *Hunt* forward into registered land. Insofar as the person in actual occupation must have an interest in land, s70(1)(g) and *Hunt* are the same. Similarly both recognise that the presence of the vendor on the land does not exclude the possibility of occupation by another. In *Hunt* the occupation was that of the lessee, in *Boland* it was that of the wife although Lord Wilberforce said that the rule could apply in favour of any person in actual occupation.

However, there are marked differences. Whereas *Hunt* is based on, and requires some investigation of the land, s70(1)(g) will bind a purchaser whether he knows of the existence of the right or not and whether he could have discovered it or not; it does not require any search or investigation of the land and is not in any way based on the doctrine of notice.

Secondly, like *Hunt*, if enquiry is made under s70(1)(g) and the rights are not disclosed (as a result of active concealment on the part of the person who claims them), the purchaser will take free of them. But, unlike *Hunt*, s70(1)(g) neither requires nor presupposes any enquiry being made in the first place.

Thirdly, unlike *Hunt*, the overriding interests of a person in actual occupation of land under s70(1)(g) can be overreached by a purchaser. In order to do so the purchaser must comply with the provisions of s2 LPA 1925, viz, he must take a conveyance from trustees, the interest must be of a type which is capable of being overreached and he must pay the capital monies to two trustees or a trust corporation: see *City of London Building Society* v *Flegg* (5) and contrast *Boland*. The fact that s70(1)(g) is capable of being overreached serves to highlight the fact that a search or investigation of the land is not pre-supposed for the purposes of that section.

Fourthly, s70(1)(g) protects not just the person in actual occupation but also the recipient of rents and profits from the land. In this respect it is wider than the rule in *Hunt*.

Therefore there is limited truth in the statement. Both *Hunt* and s70(1)(g) deal with the interests of a person in occupation, but the former is rooted in the doctrine of notice – the latter is not and is capable of being avoided by way of overreaching.

References
(1)   [1901] 1 Ch 45
(2)   [1973] 1 WLR 1071
(3)   [1981] AC 487
(4)   [1965] Ch 958
(5)   [1988] AC 54

Question 6

Old Mr Jones, feeling that he would not be able to look after himself for very many more years, wrote to Mary, his unmarried daughter, suggesting that she come and live near him. He offered to buy her a flat to live in. Mary accepted the offer; she gave up her job and her council flat and moved into the flat her father had bought for her. The flat was conveyed into her father's name and he paid the whole of the purchase price. When Mary suggested that she would like the flat to be in her name, he dismissed the idea as absurd because, as he said, 'I am leaving everything to you in my will anyway'. Mr Jones paid all the outgoings on the flat and Mary paid nothing for the use of the flat. Mary found a part-time job and visited her father daily. This arrangement continued happily for two years when Mr Jones died, leaving all his estate to charity. Now his executors seek possession of the flat.

Advise Mary.

Would your advice be any different if Mary had provided one-tenth of the purchase price of the flat?

Suggested Solution to Question 6

General comment
A question involving the acquisition of a beneficial interest in land. A good knowledge of resulting and constructive trusts and the principles of proprietary estoppel is needed. Candidates attempting this question should be able to demonstrate a good grasp of the relevant principles and authorities, and the ability to apply them to the facts. It is important to structure the answer in a logical and coherent fashion.

Skeleton solution
- Declaration of trust in conveyance – *Goodman* v *Gallant*.

- Constructive or resulting trusts – express informal agreement – *Eves* v *Eves* and *Cooke* v *Head* – direct financial contributions.

- Proprietary estoppel – *Lloyds Bank* v *Rosset*; *Re Basham* and *Grant* v *Edwards*.

Suggested solution
In order for Mary to claim an interest in the flat she will have to look to equity for assistance. Mary is not on the title deeds so no trust arises in her favour as in *Goodman* v *Gallant* (1). Consequently, the law relating to resulting and constructive trusts and proprietary estoppel must be considered.

In the first place it is notable that Mary has not made any direct financial contributions to the purchase of the flat, whether by way of deposit or instalments. Her father provided all the purchase monies and therefore Mary cannot claim an interest based on an imputed intention that she should have an interest: see Lord Bridge in *Lloyds Bank* v *Rosset* (2).

Mary could seek to argue that she has an interest by virtue of express informal agreement at the date of acquisition (or exceptionally later) with her father, which she has acted upon to her detriment (see Lord Bridge in *Rosset*). It is unclear whether the father made the statement at the time of buying the flat or later, but it may be possible to assert that his response to Mary's request to put the property into her name ('I'm leaving everything to you anyway') is evidence of such an agreement as was recognised in *Cooke* v *Head* (3) and *Eves* v *Eves* (4). In the former case the man said that the woman's name should not appear on the title deeds as it might prejudice her pending divorce, and in the latter because she was too young. In both cases the Court of Appeal took the view that the statements were evidence of an intention that the women should have an interest. If *Cooke* and *Eves* are followed, Mary will have an interest which is determined according to the agreement and not in proportion to any contribution she may have made.

In order to succeed in such a plea Mary would have to establish not only the existence of the agreement but also that she acted to her detriment on it. The most common form of detriment is a material sacrifice in the nature of financial contributions or improvements to property. On the facts Mary has not acted to her detriment in either of these ways and it is a moot point whether she has acted to her detriment in giving up her job and council flat, so as to raise a constructive trust in her favour. It could be argued that the giving up of the council flat is connected with the alleged agreement (*Grant* v *Edwards* (5)) but, the giving up of the job may not be related to the agreement at all but may have been the result of Mary's love and affection for her father.

Should Mary fail to establish an interest under a constructive trust she may be able to rely on a proprietary estoppel – a point which was specifically recognised by Lord Bridge in *Rosset* where he approved *Grant* and *Re Basham* (6). Mary would have to show that there was a representation that she would receive an interest, then or in the future: *Re Basham*. For these purposes her father's statement would suffice. Additionally, Mary would have to show that she acted to her detriment in reliance on that statement. Therefore, the date when the statement was made is all important. Assuming that the statement preceded Mary leaving her flat and job, those acts could be seen as acts of detriment: see *Jones* v *Jones* (7). Mary's acts of visiting her father are likely to be seen as the acts of a loving and caring daughter and not acts of detriment. Should the father's statement have come after Mary gave up her job and flat, those acts cannot be seen as acts *in reliance on* that statement, and an estoppel will not arise.

On balance, it seems unlikely that Mary can plead that a resulting or constructive trust has arisen in her favour, but it may be possible for her to show that an estoppel has arisen which binds everyone except the bona fide purchaser: *Inwards* v *Baker* (8).

If Mary had provided one-tenth of the purchase price

If Mary had provided one-tenth of the purchase price, in the absence of evidence to show that it was a gift to her father, she would acquire an interest in the property, proportionate to her contribution, by virtue of a resulting trust by way of direct financial contribution referable to acquisition.

References
(1)   [1986] Fam 106
(2)   [1990] 2 WLR 867
(3)   [1972] 1 WLR 518
(4)   [1975] 1 WLR 1338
(5)   [1986] Ch 638
(6)   [1986] 1 WLR 1498
(7)   [1977] 1 WLR 438
(8)   [1965] 2 QB 29

Question 7

Alan owned Blackacre and the adjoining Whiteacre, and in 1960 he sold Blackacre to Douglas who covenanted with Alan and his successors-in-title a) not to let the property fall into disrepair and b) not to use the property for business purposes.

On the assumption that the land is unregistered, consider how far these covenants will be enforceable

a) by a lessee of Whiteacre against Douglas;

b) by Alan against an adverse possessor of Blackacre; and

c) by a purchaser of Whiteacre against a purchaser of Blackacre.

Suggested Solution to Question 7

General comment
Not a difficult question for the candidate who is well-prepared. An understanding of how covenants affect successors-in-title other than purchasers is essential. The principles of registration must also be considered.

Skeleton solution
*   Definition of restrictive covenant.

*   Running of benefit to covenantee's successor – common law rules – *Smith & Snipes Hall Farm* v *River Douglas Catchment Board* – s78 LPA 1925.

*   Limitation Act 1980.

*   *Re Nisbet & Potts' Contract* – annexation – *Mill Lodge Properties Ltd.*

*   Running of benefit to covenantee's successor in equity – annexation – assignment – building scheme.

*   Running of burden to covenantor's successor – *Tulk* v *Moxhay*.

*   Registration.

*   Section 84 LPA 1925.

Suggested solution
A restrictive covenant is an agreement under seal whereby one party (the covenantor) agrees with another party (the covenantee) that he (the covenantor) will, or will not, do certain acts in relation to a defined area of land. The land owned by the covenantee will have the benefit of the covenant and that owned by the covenantor will have the burden. On the facts Alan, who owns Whiteacre, is the covenantee and Douglas, who owns Blackacre, is the covenantor.

Covenant (a) is a positive covenant because it requires the covenantor, or his successors, to maintain and repair Blackacre. Covenant (b) is negative in that it simply prohibits the use of Blackacre for business purposes.

a) *Lessee of Whiteacre*
   A lessee of Whiteacre would be a successor-in-title to the original covenantee (Alan). In order to be able to enforce the covenants against

Douglas (the original covenantor) the lessee must have obtained the benefit of the covenants. This he can do under the common law rules governing the running of the benefit. At common law four conditions have to be complied with in order for the benefit to run. Firstly, the covenants must 'touch and concern' the land. In *Smith & Snipes Hall Farm* v *River Douglas Catchment Board* (1) this was said to be satisfied if the covenants affected mode of occupation, or directly affected the value of land. Covenant (b) clearly affects mode of occupation and (a) affects value. Secondly, the original covenantee must have had a legal estate in land. In this case Alan did have a legal estate in Whiteacre, presumably in the nature of fee simple.

Thirdly, the successor to the covenantee must have a legal estate in land, although not necessarily the same legal estate. This is also satisfied because the lessee would have a legal term of years in the land. In any event this requirement has been abrogated by s78 Law of Property Act (LPA) 1925 which states that a covenant relating to land of the covenantee shall be deemed to be made with the covenantee *and his successors-in-title and the persons deriving title under him or them*, and so extends to a lessee of the covenantee. Fourthly, there must be an intention that the covenants should run with the land. This too is covered by s78 which provides that such an intention is deemed to be present and does not admit of a contrary intention.

If the conditions are satisfied the benefit of both the positive covenant (a) and the negative one (b), will have run to the lessee enabling him to enforce them against Douglas.

It should be noted that it is not necessary to show that the burden of the covenants has run to Douglas as he is the original covenantor. Neither is it necessary to deal with registration because that would only be relevant when dealing with a purchaser of the burdened land (Blackacre).

b) *Adverse possessor of Blackacre*

An adverse possessor of Blackacre will have obtained Blackacre under the Limitation Act 1980, by showing 12 years' possession adverse to the paper owner (Douglas). In running up that time the adverse possessor must show factual possession and the intention to possess.

As the adverse possessor is not a purchaser of the servient land (Blackacre) he will be bound by any covenants which are annexed to the land: *Re Nisbet & Potts' Contract* (2). This applies to both positive and negative covenants whether they are registered as D(ii) land charges or not. The covenants could be shown to be annexed in two ways, firstly, by way of express annexation and, secondly, by virtue of s78.

Express annexation will occur if certain conditions are satisfied. It must be possible to identify the land to be benefited from the wording of the covenants. In *Rogers* v *Hosegood* (3) the covenant was deemed to be annexed as it referred to the dominant land; however, in *Renals* v *Cowlishaw* (4) the covenant was not annexed because it referred solely to 'heirs, executors, administrators and assigns'. It is not clear from the limited facts whether the dominant land is capable of being identified from the covenants themselves. Where the dominant land is sold off in plots it is also necessary to show that the covenants were annexed to each and every part of the estate rather than to the estate as a whole: *Re Selwyn's Conveyance* (5). This is not the case here. It would also appear from *Re Ballard's Conveyance* (6), that annexation can only occur where substantially the whole of the dominant land is capable of benefitting. There is nothing to suggest that Whiteacre is so large as to prevent this happening.

Alternatively, s78 LPA could operate to annex the covenants to the land. In *Federated Homes* v *Mill Lodge Properties Ltd* (7) the court held that a covenant could be annexed to land by virtue of the section where the dominant land was identifiable and the covenants touched and concerned the land as per *Smith & Snipes*.

Consequently, provided there is effective annexation, Alan, the original covenantee, can enforce both covenants against the adverse possessor of Blackacre.

c) *A purchaser of Whiteacre and a purchaser of Blackacre*

In order for a purchaser of Whiteacre from Alan to enforce the covenants against a purchaser of Blackacre from Douglas, it must be shown that the benefit of the covenants has run to the former and the burden to the latter.

The purchaser of Whiteacre will be a successor-in-title to the covenantee, and the benefit of the covenants could run to him at common law or equity. The running of the benefit at common law has been dealt with in part a) above. This is not likely to be a successful way of enforcing the covenant as, with very limited exceptions (eg chain of indemnity covenants, long leases), the burden of covenants does not run at common law.

Consequently, it will be better for the purchaser to show that benefit and burden have run in equity. The benefit of the covenants can run in equity in four different ways, namely, annexation, assignment, building scheme and under s78 LPA 1925.

Annexation and s78 have already been dealt with under part b) above. Assignment is the process of transferring the benefit of the covenant to the covenantee's successor. In order for this to be achieved it has to be shown that the dominant land (Whiteacre) can be identified, directly or indirectly, in the assignment (see *Newton Abbot Co-operative Society* v *Williamson & Treadgold* (8)), secondly, that the assignment was contemporaneous with transfer or conveyance, and thirdly, that there was a clear intention to assign.

A building scheme or scheme of development is governed by the rules laid down in *Elliston* v *Reacher* (9), as amended: see *Re Dolphin's Conveyance* (10) and *Baxter* v *Four Oaks Properties Ltd* (11). Those rules require an intention on the part of the vendor to set up a building scheme in relation to a defined area of land. As long as that intention is manifest, the purchasers buy subject to the scheme of covenants which crystallises upon the first purchase. Under the scheme each purchaser can enforce, and have enforced against him, the negative covenants which make up the scheme.

Provided one of the four methods discussed above can be satisfied, the benefit of the covenants will have run to the purchaser of Whiteacre in equity.

The running of the burden of the covenants to the purchaser of Blackacre in equity is governed by the rule in *Tulk* v *Moxhay* (12). Under *Tulk* four conditions have to be satisfied. Firstly, the covenants must touch and concern the land as per *Smith & Snipes* (discussed above). Secondly, the covenants must be negative in substance. Equity will not enforce positive covenants against a successor-in-title to the covenantor. The test to determine whether a covenant is negative is the 'hand in pocket test': *Haywood* v *Brunswick Permanent Benefit Building Society* (13). If the covenant requires the covenantor to expend money it is positive and cannot be enforced against a successor-in-title. On the facts covenant (a) is positive and cannot be enforced against the purchaser of Blackacre from Douglas.

Thirdly, at the time the covenant was made the original covenantee must have retained land capable of benefitting from it. On the facts when the covenant was made in 1960 Alan, the original covenantee, retained land capable of benefitting (Whiteacre). Fourthly, there must have been an intention that the burden should run. This is provided for by s79 LPA 1925; in the absence of contrary intention the covenantor is deemed to covenant on behalf of himself and successors.

If these four factors are present the burden of covenant (b) will have run to the purchaser of Blackacre in equity. However, it is not enough to show that benefit and burden have run in equity – in order to be enforceable against the purchaser of Blackacre it must be shown that covenant (b) was properly protected by the registration of a D(ii) land charge by Alan (the original covenantee), against the name of Douglas (the original covenantor). If it was, the purchaser of Blackacre will be bound by it; if not, he will take free of it: see *Midland Bank* v *Green* (14).

Even if benefit and burden have run in equity and covenant (b) was registered as a D(ii) charge, the purchaser of Blackacre may be able to rely on s84 LPA 1925 to modify or discharge the covenant. This can be done if he can show one of the following grounds: that the covenant is obsolete due to changes in the character of the neighbourhood, that it impedes the reasonable development of land, that it could be discharged without adversely affecting the covenantee or his successors, or there is agreement to do so.

References
(1)   [1949] 2 KB 500
(2)   [1905] 1 Ch 391
(3)   [1900] 2 Ch 388
(4)   (1878) 9 Ch D 125
(5)   [1967] Ch 674
(6)   [1937] Ch 473
(7)   [1980] 1 WLR 594
(8)   [1952] Ch 286
(9)   [1908] 2 Ch 374
(10) [1970] Ch 654
(11) [1965] Ch 816
(12) (1848) 2 Ph 774
(13) (1881) 8 QBD 403
(14) [1981] 2 WLR 28

Question 8

Mike, Pat, Rob and Saul formed a pop group and decided to buy a house together situated near the recording studios. All four of them contributed equally to the purchase price and the house was conveyed into the joint names of Mike, Pat and Rob; Saul was aged 17 at the time of the conveyance. The pop group was not a success and in 1990 Mike sold his interest in the house to Pat. Shortly afterwards Rob wrote to Pat offering to sell him his interest for a certain price. Pat replied that he would be happy to purchase Rob's interest, but that the price was too high. Before any negotiations took place Rob was killed in a motor accident. Saul now wishes the house to be sold whereas Pat wishes to continue living there.

Saul would like to know whether he can force a sale of the house and, if so, how the proceeds would be divided.

Advise Saul.

Suggested Solution to Question 8

General comment
A fairly straightforward question on severance of a joint tenancy and the operation of s30 LPA 1925. The only 'tricky' part lies in the fact that one joint tenant sells to another, so that that other remains a joint tenant of his original share and becomes a tenant-in-common in respect of his 'new share'.

Skeleton solution
* Co-ownership trust for sale – s34–36 LPA 1925.

* Joint tenancy – four unities – contributions.

* Severance – *Williams* v *Hensman*.

* Sale to existing joint tenant – *Re Mayo*.

* Section 30 LPA 1925 application for order for sale – secondary or collateral trusts – *Jones* v *Challenger*.

Suggested solution
Whenever two or more people contribute to the purchase of property which is not conveyed into all of their names, the Law of Property Act (LPA) 1925 brings into play a trust for sale in favour of the co-owners.

Mike, Pat, Rob and Saul contribute equally to the purchase of the house, and they are thus co-owners. As Saul is a minor he cannot hold the legal estate (s1(6) LPA 1925), and so the house is conveyed into the names of Mike, Pat and Rob who hold it on trust for sale for themselves and Saul in equity (ss34–36 LPA 1925). The legal estate is held by the three of them as joint tenants as a tenancy-in-common cannot exist at law.

All four hold the equitable interests as joint tenants for the following reasons. Firstly, the four unities (possession, interest, time and title) appear to be present as all of them are entitled to possess and occupy the house, all of them have the same interest (presumably fee simple), they all acquired that interest at the same time, namely, the date of conveyance, and they all acquired it under the same act or document, viz, the purchase of the house. Secondly, they have contributed equally to the purchase in which case equity presumes a joint tenancy. Thirdly, the house is purchased to be lived in, it is not purchased as a business asset or as business premises (see *Malayan Credit* v *Jack Chia* (1), although it will enable them to get to the recording studio easier.

53

As they are joint tenants none of them can point to a specific share of the property as being theirs – they each own the entirety, although upon sale they will each be entitled to a quarter share of the proceeds. Moreover, as there is a joint tenancy the doctrine of survivorship operates so that, unless a joint tenant has severed his interest during life, his interest passes to the other joint tenants on his death.

The interests of the four could be expressed as follows:

Mike	Pat	Rob		Legal Title (Joint Tenants)
Mike	Pat	Rob	Saul	Equity
JT	JT	JT	JT	
$\frac{1}{4}$	$\frac{1}{4}$	$\frac{1}{4}$	$\frac{1}{4}$	

A joint tenancy can be severed by a joint tenant acting upon his 'share', eg by selling it. In fact the tenancy will have been severed the moment Mike entered into a specifically enforceable contract of sale with Pat. The transaction has no effect on the legal title and Mike remains a trustee for sale. As far as the equitable interests are concerned, Mike drops out of the picture and is no longer a beneficiary behind the trust for sale. Pat will remain a joint tenant in equity of his original interest vis-a-vis Rob and Saul, and will have become a tenant-in-common in respect of the share he has acquired from Mike. He cannot be a joint tenant in respect of this share because unity of title is missing.

The interests of the parties can now be expressed as follows:

Mike	Pat	Rob		Legal Title (Joint Tenants)
Mike	Pat	Rob	Saul	Equity
(TIC)	JT	JT	JT	
$\left(\frac{1}{4}\right)$	$\frac{1}{4}$	$\frac{1}{4}$	$\frac{1}{4}$	

Although a joint tenancy can be severed by way of mutual agreement or mutual conduct (see *Williams* v *Hensman* (2), neither could be said to have occurred here, as the price had not been agreed (contrast: *Burgess* v *Rawnsley* (3)). The letter then has no effect on either the legal or beneficial interests.

Rob's death does not effect a severance of his interest in the house, but rather survivorship operates and his share passes to the two remaining joint tenants, Pat and Saul. The legal estate is now vested in Mike and Pat as trustees for sale on trust for Saul and Pat as joint tenants of their original shares and the share of Rob which has passed to them by survivorship, and Pat as tenant-in-common in respect of the share he purchased from Mike, viz:

Mike	Pat		Legal Title (Joint Tenants)
Pat	Pat	Saul	Equity
(TIC)	JT	JT	
$\left(\frac{2}{8}\right)$	$\frac{3}{8}$	$\frac{3}{8}$	

By definition, trustees of a trust for sale must sell. That notwithstanding, s25 LPA 1925 gives trustees a power to postpone sale provided that they act unanimously – in the absence of unanimity the duty to sell prevails: *Re Mayo* (4). Hence, Mike and Pat can agree to postpone sale. It would not avail Saul to rely on s26(3) LPA 1925 as that section only requires the trustees to consult the beneficiaries, and where practicable, give effect to the wishes of the majority. On the facts Pat has the majority interest $\left(\frac{5}{8}\right)$, and anyway the trustees only have to consult not obey.

Saul could make an application to the court under s30 LPA 1925 for an order for sale, as he is clearly an interested party for the purposes of that section. In deciding whether or not to order sale the court will consider whether there was a secondary or collateral purpose to the trust, and whether that purpose still exists. If it does, sale will not be ordered: see *Jones* v *Challenger* (5); *Re Buchanan-Wollaston's Conveyance* (6). It could be argued that the secondary or collateral purpose lay in the fact that the purchase of the house was connected to the four's membership of the pop group and as the group has since disbanded, the secondary purpose has ceased to exist and sale should be ordered.

If sale is ordered pursuant to s30 LPA 1925 Saul will receive $\frac{3}{8}$ and Pat $\frac{5}{8}$ of the proceeds.

References
(1)   [1986] AC 549
(2)   (1861) 1 John & H 546
(3)   [1975] Ch 429
(4)   [1943] Ch 302
(5)   [1961] 1 QB 176
(6)   [1939] Ch 738

HLT PUBLICATIONS

All HLT Publications have two important qualities. First, they are written by specialists, all of whom have direct practical experience of teaching the syllabus. Second, all Textbooks are reviewed and updated each year to reflect new developments and changing trends. They are used widely by students at polytechnics and colleges throughout the United Kingdom and overseas.

A comprehensive range of titles is covered by the following classifications.

- **TEXTBOOKS**
- **CASEBOOKS**
- **SUGGESTED SOLUTIONS**
- **REVISION WORKBOOKS**

The books listed overleaf should be available from your local bookshop. In case of difficulty, however, they can be obtained direct from the publisher using this order form. Telephone, Fax or Telex orders will also be accepted. Quote your Access, Visa or American Express card numbers for priority orders. To order direct from publisher please enter cost of titles you require, fill in despatch details and send it with your remittance to The HLT Group Ltd. **Please complete the order form overleaf.**

DETAILS FOR DESPATCH OF PUBLICATIONS
Please insert your full name below

Please insert below the style in which you would like the correspondence from the Publisher addressed to you
TITLE Mr, Miss etc.   INITIALS   SURNAME/FAMILY NAME

Address to which study material is to be sent (please ensure someone will be present to accept delivery of your Publications).

POSTAGE & PACKING
You are welcome to purchase study material from the Publisher at 200 Greyhound Road, London W14 9RY, during normal working hours.

If you wish to order by post this may be done direct from the Publisher. Postal charges are as follows:

UK   – Orders over £30: no charge. Orders below £30: £2.60. Single paper (last exam only): 55p
OVERSEAS   – See table below

The Publisher cannot accept responsibility in respect of postal delays or losses in the postal systems.
DESPATCH All cheques must be cleared before material is despatched.

SUMMARY OF ORDER   Date of order:

Add postage and packing: Cost of publications ordered:
                                                  UNITED KINGDOM:

OVERSEAS:	TEXTS		Suggested Solutions (Last exam only)	
	One	Each Extra		
Eire	£5.00	£0.70	£1.00	
European Community	£10.50	£1.00	£1.00	
East Europe & North America	£12.50	£1.50	£1.50	
South East Asia	£12.00	£2.00	£1.50	
Australia/New Zealand	£14.00	£3.00	£1.70	
Other Countries (Africa, India etc)	£13.00	£3.00	£1.50	

Total cost of order: £

Please ensure that you enclose a cheque or draft payable to
THE HLT GROUP LTD for the above amount, or charge to ☐ Access ☐ Visa ☐ American Express

Card Number

Expiry Date .... Signature ....

LLB PUBLICATIONS	TEXTBOOKS Cost £	£	CASEBOOKS Cost £	£	REVISION WORKBOOKS Cost £	£	SUG. SOL 1986/91 Cost £	£	SUG. SOL 1992 Cost £	£
Administrative Law	£18.95		£19.95				£9.95		£3.00	
Commercial Law Vol I	£18.95		£19.95		£9.95		£9.95		£3.00	
Commercial Law Vol II	£17.95		£19.95							
Company Law	£19.95		£19.95		£9.95		£9.95		£3.00	
Conflict of Laws	£18.95		£17.95		£9.95					
Constitutional Law	£16.95		£17.95		£9.95		£9.95		£3.00	
Contract Law	£16.95		£17.95		£9.95		£9.95		£3.00	
Conveyancing	£19.95		£17.95							
Criminal Law	£16.95		£18.95		£9.95		£9.95		£3.00	
Criminology	£17.95						£4.95†		£3.00	
English Legal System	£16.95		£14.95		£9.95		£8.95*		£3.00	
European Community Law	£17.95		£19.95		£9.95		£4.95†		£3.00	
Equity and Trusts	£16.95		£17.95		£9.95					
Evidence	£19.95		£18.95		£9.95		£9.95		£3.00	
Family Law	£18.95		£19.95		£9.95		£9.95		£3.00	
Jurisprudence	£16.95				£9.95		£9.95		£3.00	
Land Law	£16.95		£17.95		£9.95		£9.95		£3.00	
Law of Trusts							£9.95		£3.00	
Public International Law	£18.95		£18.95		£9.95		£9.95		£3.00	
Revenue Law	£19.95		£19.95		£9.95		£9.95		£3.00	
Roman Law	£14.95									
Succession	£19.95		£18.95		£9.95		£9.95		£3.00	
Tort	£16.95		£17.95		£9.95		£9.95		£3.00	

BAR PUBLICATIONS

	TEXTBOOKS Cost £	£	CASEBOOKS Cost £	£	REVISION WORKBOOKS Cost £	£	SUG. SOL 1986/91 Cost £	£	SUG. SOL 1992 Cost £	£
Conflict of Laws	£18.95		£17.95				£9.95§		£4.50	
Civil & Criminal Procedure	£21.95		£20.95				£14.95		£4.50	
European Community Law & Human Rights	£17.95		£19.95				£9.95§		£4.50	
Evidence	£19.95		£18.95				£14.95		£4.50	
Family Law	£18.95		£19.95				£14.95		£4.50	
General Paper I	£21.95		£20.95				£14.95		£4.50	
General Paper II	£21.95		£20.95				£14.95		£4.50	
Law of International Trade	£17.95		£19.95				£14.95		£4.50	
Practical Conveyancing	£19.95		£17.95				£14.95		£4.50	
Revenue Law	£19.95		£19.95				£14.95		£4.50	
Sale of Goods & Credit	£18.95		£18.95				£14.95		£4.50	

LAW SOCIETY FINALS	TEXTBOOKS		REVISION WORKBOOKS		SUGGESTED SOLUTIONS to Summer & Winter Examinations for all 7 Papers	
Accounts	£14.95		£9.95		Final Exam Papers (Set) (All Papers) Summer 1989	£9.95
Business Organisations & Insolvency	£14.95				Final Exam Papers (Set) (All Papers) Winter 1990	£9.95
Consumer Protection & Employment Law	£14.95				Final Exam Papers (Set) (All Papers) Summer 1990	£9.95
Conveyancing I & II	£14.95					
Family Law	£14.95				Final Exam Papers (Set) (All Papers) Winter 1991	£9.95
Litigation	£14.95					
Wills, Probate & Administration	£14.95		£9.95		Final Exam Papers (Set) (All Papers) Summer 1991	£9.95

CPE PUBLICATIONS	TEXTBOOKS		CASEBOOKS	
Criminal Law	£16.95		£18.95	
Constitutional & Administrative Law	£16.95		£17.95	
Contract Law	£16.95		£17.95	
Equity & Trusts	£16.95		£17.95	
Land Law	£16.95		£17.95	
Tort	£16.95		£17.95	

INSTITUTE OF LEGAL EXECUTIVES	TEXTBOOKS	
Company & Partnership Law	£18.95	
Constitutional Law	£13.95	
Contract Law	£13.95	
Criminal Law	£13.95	
Equity & Trusts	£13.95	
European Law & Practice	£17.95	
Evidence	£17.95	
Land Law	£13.95	
Tort	£13.95	

*1987-1991
†1990-1991
§1988-1991